W9-BQS-292

THE ZODIAC KILLER

TERROR AND MYSTERY

true crime
WITHDRAWN

THE ZODIAC KILLER
TERROR AND MYSTERY

by Brenda Haugen

Content Adviser: Phillip Edney, Public Affairs Specialist, Federal Bureau of Investigation, Washington, D.C.

Reading Adviser: Alexa L. Sandmann, EdD, Professor of Literacy, College and Graduate School of Education, Health, and Human Services, Kent State University

Compass Point Books
151 Good Counsel Drive
P.O. Box 669
Mankato, MN 56002-0669
877-845-8392
www.capstonepub.com

 This book was manufactured with paper containing
at least 10 percent post-consumer waste.

Editor: Angie Kaelberer
Designers: Tracy Davies and Gene Bentdahl
Media Researcher: Marcie Spence
Library Consultant: Kathleen Baxter
Production Specialist: Jane Klenk

Library of Congress Cataloging-in-Publication Data
Haugen, Brenda.
  The Zodiac killer : terror and mystery / by Brenda Haugen.
   p. cm. — (True crime)
  Includes bibliographical references and index.
  ISBN 978-0-7565-4357-0 (library binding)
  1. Serial murder investigation—California—Case studies—
Juvenile literature. 2. Serial murders—California—Case studies—
Juvenile literature. 3. Serial murderers—California—Juvenile
literature. I. Title. II. Series.
  HV8079.H6H38 2011
  364.152'32097946—dc22   2010011205

Printed in the United States of America in Stevens Point, Wisconsin.
102010 005990R

HE CALLED HIMSELF "ZODIAC".

Few crimes are so shocking or so terrifying that the stories of what happened live on years, or even decades, after the offenses occurred. The shock waves from these crimes often ripple beyond the areas where they happened, fascinating and frightening entire nations—and sometimes the world. Some of these crimes are solved. Often they are not. But even when the cases grow cold, the evidence remains and awakens the amateur detective in all of us.

TABLE OF CONTENTS

CHAPTER 1

GRUESOME SHOW

It was late in the evening of October 11, 1969. In the Presidio Heights neighborhood of San Francisco, California, a 14-year-old girl looked out from a second-story window in her home. A taxi was parked across the street, about 50 feet (15 m) away. From the window, the girl could see two men in the front seat of the taxi. The street was too dark for her to tell what they were doing, but she had a feeling something bad was happening.

The girl called to her 16-year-old brother, who was hanging out with his friends. He and their younger brother joined their sister at the window. They saw a husky man holding the cabdriver's head on his lap. He seemed to be going through the man's clothing. The siblings couldn't tell whether the man was struggling with the driver or searching him. Either way, it was weird. They called the police.

San Francisco cabdriver Paul Stine was murdered on a quiet neighborhood street.

HE'D KILLED BEFORE AND OUTWITTED THE POLICE EVERY TIME.

As the kids continued to watch, the man leaned over the driver and appeared to be wiping down the inside of the taxi. By now the other teens had come to the window. The man got out of the cab and wiped down the driver's side door and the passenger door behind it. The teenagers didn't realize that the man had fired a fatal shot into driver Paul Stine's head. The killer then took Stine's wallet and cut off a piece of the driver's bloody shirt.

The killer opened the driver's side door and wiped down the dashboard again. Then he closed the door and walked away. Nothing about his behavior suggested that he feared being caught. He had reason to be confident. He'd killed before and outwitted the police every time.

CHAPTER 2

THE FIRST VICTIMS

Nearly a year before Paul Stine was shot, two California teenagers were getting ready for a Friday night date. It was December 20, 1968.

Seventeen-year-old David Faraday thought Betty Lou Jensen was cute. The 16-year-old girl went to Hogan High School, just a few blocks from her home in Vallejo, California. She was a good student and popular with her classmates. David attended Vallejo High School across town, where he was a good athlete and an even better student.

David left home at 7:30 p.m. in his mom's 1961 station wagon. It took him about a half hour to get to Betty's house.

Betty wore a purple minidress. A ribbon adorned her long brown hair. She told her parents that she and David were going to a concert at her school and then to a party. She kissed her dad good-bye and said she'd be home by 11 p.m.

For some reason the pair changed their plans. Instead of going to the concert, the couple visited one of Betty's friends. After spending about a half

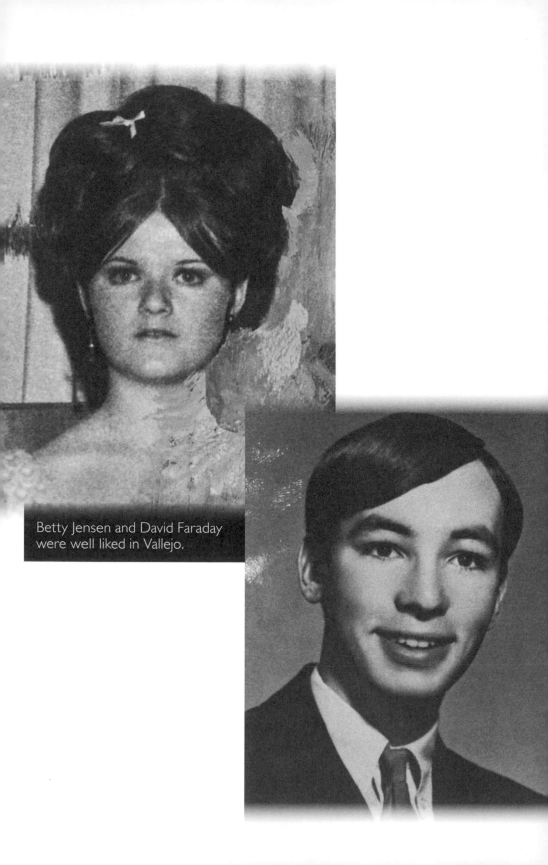

Betty Jensen and David Faraday were well liked in Vallejo.

hour there, they stopped at a drive-in restaurant called Mr. Ed's.

Afterward David and Betty drove to a remote lovers' lane on Lake Herman Road, a few miles east of the Vallejo city limits. After parking in a clearing just off the main road, David locked the car's doors and tilted the front seat back. Headlights from cars winding along Lake Herman Road brightened the darkness as they passed. But one driver did not pass. He drove off the road and stopped a few yards from the station wagon. It was just after 11 p.m., the time Betty had promised her dad she'd be home.

The driver of the other car got out of his vehicle. Evidence found later indicated that he shot out the right rear passenger window of David's car and then shot the left rear tire. As the young couple tried to climb out the front passenger side door, the man went around the car toward them. Betty got out of the car and ran toward the road. David was still in the car as the man shot him behind his left ear.

The man then turned his attention to Betty, shooting her five times in the back. She died less than

30 feet (9 m) from the station wagon. The killer got back in his car and left.

At 11:10 p.m. Stella Borges was headed for nearby Benicia to pick up her son when she came upon the grisly scene on Lake Herman Road. Frightened, she didn't stop, but decided to go for help. She kept driving until she spotted a Benicia police car a few minutes later. She honked her car's horn and blinked its headlights to get the officers' attention. Borges told Captain Daniel Pitta and Officer William Warner what she'd seen on Lake Herman Road. Their car's blue lights flashing, the officers rushed to the scene. They found David still alive. The officers called for an ambulance and began examining the scene. One of them covered Betty's lifeless body with a blanket.

The killer's car had left no tire tracks in the frozen ground. There was no sign of a struggle. The officers found a spent .22-caliber casing on the right front floorboard of the car. Reconstructing the crime, the officers decided that the killer fired 10 shots, but they discovered only eight spent casings.

THE NEWS OF DAVID'S AND BETTY'S DEATHS SHOCKED EVERYONE WHO KNEW THEM.

The police found little additional evidence, aside from a few faint footprints. Borges said she had seen a light-colored Chevrolet, which might have been the killer's car, but it wasn't much to go on. The police hoped to get more information from David, but he died before the ambulance reached the hospital.

The news of David's and Betty's deaths shocked everyone who knew them. Why, they wondered, would anyone want to kill these two well-liked teens? At the time, no one realized that the killer didn't know or care who his victims were.

CHAPTER 3

INDEPENDENCE DAY MURDER

Waitress Bobbie Ramos remembers her co-worker, Darlene Ferrin, telling her that she knew both David Faraday and Betty Jensen. Ferrin added that she would never go back to Lake Herman again. Ramos wasn't sure how Ferrin knew Betty and David. Like Betty, Ferrin had attended Hogan High, but at 22, she was six years older.

It was true that Ferrin knew a lot of people. The friendly waitress was known for talking to everyone she came into contact with. She worked nights at Terry's Restaurant in Vallejo and knew many of the restaurant's customers well.

As winter turned to spring, and then to summer, Betty's and David's killer still eluded police. Soon it was July 4, Independence Day.

That afternoon Ferrin and her sister Christina dropped by Caesar's Palace Restaurant, the restaurant where Ferrin's husband, Dean, worked. The young women were on their way to Mare Island for the annual Fourth of July celebration and boat parade.

"WHAT TIME WILL YOU BE HOME?"

"What time will you be home?" Ferrin's husband asked. "I'm inviting some people from the restaurant over to our house for a little party."

Ferrin said she'd be home around 10 p.m., and he asked her to pick up some fireworks. She agreed.

When Ferrin got home that night, she changed clothes before waking her baby daughter, Deena. She was about to take her daughter's two babysitters home when the phone rang. After talking to the caller, Ferrin asked the sitters whether they would stay a while longer so she could go out to buy fireworks. The sitters said they didn't mind, and she left.

Darlene Ferrin would cross paths with Zodiac July 4, 1969.

But instead of going for fireworks, Ferrin went to see her friend Mike Mageau. The phone call she received at home was probably from him. At around 11:30 p.m., she pulled up in front of his house in her bronze Chevy Corvair. Mageau ran out of the house. He seemed to be in a hurry, because he left the door wide open and all the lights and the TV on.

After they left his house in Ferrin's car, Mageau soon realized they were being followed. Ferrin made turn after turn but couldn't shake the car behind hers. Mageau told her to turn onto Springs Road and head east to Blue Rock Springs Park in Benicia. Ferrin followed his directions and pulled into a parking lot overlooking the Blue Rock Springs Golf Course.

After turning off the car's headlights, Ferrin and Mageau sat in the darkness, listening to the radio. A vehicle similar to Ferrin's Corvair stopped near her car, paused for a while, and then sped off toward Vallejo. About five minutes later, the car returned, stopping behind Ferrin's Corvair. A man got out of the car, leaving its headlights on and carrying a bright flashlight. Thinking the man was a police officer, Mageau reached for his ID and opened his window as the man came around to his side of the car.

Before Mageau could show him his ID, the man drew a gun and fired through the open window. Mageau felt the heat of the bullets as they ripped into his face and body. He saw Ferrin slump over the steering wheel. The bullets had passed through his body and into hers. The man also fired directly at Ferrin.

In terrible pain, Mageau yelled as the man walked back to his car. Realizing he had left a victim alive, the man walked back to the Corvair and shot Mageau two more times. He fired another two shots at Ferrin before he walked back to his car and sped off.

A short time later, three teens were driving through the area looking for a friend when they came upon the scene. They saw Mageau writhing

"I REMEMBER SHE WAS TRYING TO SAY SOMETHING, AND I PUT MY EAR OVER HER... TO TRY TO UNDERSTAND, BUT I JUST COULDN'T."

on the ground. He told them he and Ferrin had been shot and needed help. The teens rushed off to call the police.

When police arrived, they saw Ferrin behind the wheel of the car, her eyes open slightly, a soft moan escaping from her lips. Two of the officers recognized her.

"Lots of cops knew her and used to stop in at the coffee shop out there where she worked," Detective Sergeant John Lynch later said. "I knew who Darlene was, but I never talked to her."

Though she was badly injured, Ferrin tried to speak to Lynch.

"I remember she was trying to say something, and I put my ear over her … to try to understand, but I just couldn't," he said.

Despite his many wounds, Mageau was able to talk. Haltingly, he told Lynch what had happened. He described the shooter as about 5 feet 8 inches (173 centimeters) tall and weighing at least 195 pounds (88 kilograms). Mageau said the shooter was a young white man and had a large face. He said he was driving a light tan car. Mageau added that the man never said a word. He just started shooting.

An ambulance quickly arrived to take Ferrin and Mageau to a hospital. Officer Richard Hoffman of the Vallejo Police Department went with the injured pair in case Ferrin could shed more light on what had happened, but that wasn't to be. She died on the way to the hospital. Mageau went right into surgery. He would survive the attack.

"I ALSO KILLED THOSE KIDS LAST YEAR."

At 12:40 a.m., two minutes after Darlene Ferrin was pronounced dead, a call came into the Vallejo Police Department reporting a double murder. To Nancy Slover, the police department operator who took the call, the caller's statement seemed rehearsed. He didn't stop talking and wouldn't let her interrupt. Slover said he sounded mature and spoke without an accent. After telling Slover where to find the bodies, the man said, "They were shot with a 9-millimeter Luger. I also killed those kids last year."

The killer's final word was delivered in a deep, taunting tone: "Good-bye." Then he hung up.

Through the phone company, police were able to trace the call. It had been placed at a pay phone—just a few blocks from the Solano County Sheriff's Office in Vallejo.

CHAPTER 4

NAME GAMES

onald Harden had loved decoding messages since he was a boy. Now a teacher at North Salinas High School, he sat down at the dining room table with the Sunday, August 3, 1969, edition of the *San Francisco Examiner-Chronicle*.

The *San Francisco Examiner*, the *Vallejo Times-Herald*, and the *San Francisco Chronicle* had received similar letters from a man claiming to be the Vallejo killer. He gave details of the murders that only the killer was likely to know. He ended each letter with the same symbol—a crossed-circle design that would become the killer's signature.

A mysterious symbol became the killer's signature.

IF THE CIPHER WAS SOLVED, THE KILLER SAID, HIS IDENTITY WOULD BE REVEALED.

He also sent each newspaper one-third of a complete cipher—a coded message. Each third of the cipher was eight lines long, and each line contained 17 symbols. If the cipher was solved, the killer said, his identity would be revealed. He said he wanted the ciphers printed on the front pages of the newspapers by August 1, 1969. If that wasn't done, he said, he would go on a killing spree. Experts with the Central Intelligence Agency, the Federal Bureau of Investigation, the Office of Naval Intelligence, and the National Security Agency tried to break the code but were unsuccessful.

The *San Francisco Examiner-Chronicle* published all three parts of the cipher in its combined August 3 edition. Donald Harden decided he would try to break the code. Using common sense, patience, and a reference book on code breaking, he went to work.

Harden looked for patterns and symbols that were repeated often. He knew that the symbol most often repeated likely represented the letter E, the most common letter in the English language. Many words end with the letter E, so this was another clue. And if two identical symbols were next to each other, they likely each stood for an E, L, or S. These are the most commonly doubled letters in the English language. Harden used these and other tidbits of knowledge to try to unravel the cipher.

Three hours after Harden began the task, his wife, Bettye, pitched in. They worked on the cipher the rest of the day. In the morning Harden was ready to give up. After watching his wife continue to work, though, he was drawn back into the mystery.

AFTER 20 HOURS OF HARD WORK, THE HARDENS HAD DECIPHERED THE CODE.

Soon letters started falling into place and making sense, but it wasn't easy. The Hardens discovered that the killer hadn't spelled all the words right or used punctuation. He also used several different symbols to represent the same letter. For instance, seven different symbols represented the letter E. Still, after 20 hours of hard work, the Hardens had deciphered the code. The first part of the message read:

I LIKE KILLING PEOPLE
BECAUSE IT IS SO MUCH
FUN IT IS MORE FUN THAN
KILLING WILD GAME IN
THE FORREST BECAUSE
MAN IS THE MOST DANGEROUE
ANAMAL OF ALL TO KILL

Donald Harden decoded most of the killer's coded message.

The message went on to explain that the killer believed that all the people he killed would become his slaves in the afterlife.

Donald Harden called the *Examiner*. The editor who took his call thought Harden was just like the hundreds of other readers who had called to say they had solved the code. But he told Harden to send his solution to the newspaper, and he would give it to Detective Sergeant Lynch.

POLICE STILL HAD NO CLUE WHO THE KILLER WAS.

My name is —

A E N ⊕ ⊗ K ⊗ M ⊙ ⅃ N A M

No one ever figured out the part of the message that supposedly gave the killer's name.

Naval intelligence analysts examined the Hardens' work and said they were right. But the killer had lied. He had said the solved cipher would reveal his identity. Now that the cipher was solved, police still had no clue who the killer was.

Not everyone believed that the killer had sent the letters to the newspapers. Vallejo Police Chief Jack Stiltz was among those who were skeptical.

HE CALLED HIMSELF "ZODIAC."

He said anyone who talked to witnesses of the murders and assaults could know details of the crime scenes. Stiltz wanted more proof from the killer and publicly asked him to send another letter with more details.

His request was granted August 7. That day the *Examiner* received a three-page letter from the killer that contained more details. The killer also provided something else—a nickname. He called himself "Zodiac."

CHAPTER 5

HORROR BY THE LAKE

On Sunday, September 27, 1969, Cecelia Shepard and Bryan Hartnell were relaxing in the afternoon sunshine at Lake Berryessa Recreation Area in Napa County, California. They had found a secluded spot on Twin Oak Ridge, a peninsula on the lake's western shore, where they could be alone.

The lake outing had been a spur-of-the-moment decision. Shepard and Hartnell had been friends since they were freshmen at Pacific Union College in Angwin, California. Now, two years later, Shepard was transferring to the University of California at Riverside. After they'd attended church together, they had boxed up her belongings and walked to the Pacific Union cafeteria.

During lunch Hartnell asked Shepard whether she had any plans for the afternoon. He suggested that they drive to San Francisco. They took off in his white Volkswagen Karmann Ghia. With no definite plans, the couple stopped at a garage sale, did a little shopping in the town of St. Helena, and visited

Cecelia Shepard and Bryan Hartnell had dated during college.

friends. Because it was by then late in the day, they decided San Francisco was too far away. Hartnell had another idea.

"There's this one place, a favorite of mine where I used to go all the time," he said.

The place was beautiful Lake Berryessa, a large manmade lake filled with enough fish to keep almost any angler happy. At 4 p.m. the young couple found the parking lot deserted. Twin Oak Ridge, a quarter-mile (400-meter) walk past a pair of tall oaks, also was free of people.

The couple sat down on a blanket. They enjoyed the view of the lake and each other's company. As twilight neared, something else caught Shepard's eye. A heavyset, dark-haired man dressed in dark clothing was approaching. He appeared to be between 5 feet 8 inches (173 cm) and 6 feet (183 cm) tall and was wearing glasses.

The man disappeared into a grove of trees about 250 yards (229 m) away. Because of the man's odd behavior—he had seemed to be watching them—Shepard kept her eyes on the grove of trees. When the man re-emerged, Shepard told Hartnell they weren't alone anymore.

Unconcerned, Hartnell remained lying on the blanket. Shepard rested her head on his shoulder. The man drew closer and closer, ducking behind one of the two oak trees the couple had passed on

Lake Berryessa was a popular recreation area.

their way to Twin Oak Ridge. Behind the tree, the man put on an unusual costume. Over his head was a hood, with holes for his eyes and mouth. Clip-on sunglasses covered his eyes. The hood flowed down nearly to the man's waist, looking somewhat like a bib. On the front of the bib was a sewn version of Zodiac's signature—a cross extending from inside a circle.

On the left side of his belt, the man carried a 12-inch (30-cm) knife in a wooden sheath. On his right side was an empty holster. He pointed a pistol at Shepard and Hartnell as he walked toward them, now just 20 feet (6 m) away.

"I want your money and your car keys," the man calmly said. "I want your car to go to Mexico."

Hartnell quickly handed the man his car keys and all the coins he had in his pockets. The man put the money in his pockets but dropped the car keys on the blanket. He said he was a convict and that he had killed a prison guard while escaping from a prison in Montana. He added that he had nothing to lose.

Hartnell talked to the man, hoping he would just take the keys and money and go away. Those hopes were dashed when the man removed a length of clothesline from his belt. He told Hartnell to lie facedown on the ground so he could be tied up. Hartnell ignored the man's order and stood up.

"Get down!" Zodiac yelled. "Right now!"

Hartnell thought he could grab the man's gun. Had he been alone, he likely would have tried. But he had Shepard to consider. It was one thing to take a chance with his life. He didn't want to risk hers.

After Hartnell again took his place on the blanket, the man ordered Shepard to tie up Hartnell. She obeyed, knotting the rope loosely around his hands and feet. Then the man tied her up and tightened the knots on Hartnell's hands and feet. Shepard lay on her stomach, and Hartnell was on his left side, waiting to see what the man would do next. He quietly talked to the couple for a few minutes. When Hartnell asked whether the gun was loaded, the man showed him that it was.

"I'M GOING TO HAVE TO STAB YOU PEOPLE."

The calmness of the situation quickly changed as the man pulled the knife from the sheath on his belt. Even the man's voice changed, growing deeper as he said, "I'm going to have to stab you people."

Hartnell had hoped that at the worst, they would be left tied up on the peninsula. But seeing the knife, he knew the situation was much more grim. Saying he couldn't stand to see Shepard hurt, he begged the man to stab him first. As Shepard screamed in horror, the man repeatedly stabbed Hartnell in the back. His tense body sagged. The man may have thought he was dead.

"I QUIT BREATHING! I JUST FROZE!"

Breathing heavily, the man turned to Shepard. He stabbed her several times in the back before dropping the knife. Trying to protect herself, she turned onto her back, but the man picked up the knife and continued his assault as she begged him to stop.

Hartnell was still alive. Knowing he could do nothing to save Shepard, he kept still and quiet, pretending to be dead. The man, apparently satisfied that he'd killed the couple, rose from the blanket and walked away.

"When Zodiac left he must have thought we were dead," Hartnell said later. "I was extremely fortunate to survive. I quit breathing! I just froze! What I heard was him walk away in a non-hurried fashion. And then after that there's a little dead spot I don't remember."

Shepard also survived the attack, but she and Hartnell likely passed out for a while. When they regained consciousness and realized what had happened, they gathered whatever strength they still had and yelled for help. Every movement brought terrible pain, but Hartnell managed to get his face near Shepard's hands. Using his teeth, he slowly untied her wrists. When she was free, she managed to untie the tight binding around his wrists. Hartnell hoped to crawl for help, but he'd lost so much blood that he didn't have the energy.

Fortunately for the couple, a man who was fishing with his son in a boat heard their cries and rowed closer to see what was going on. Frightened, the man and his son didn't dare rush to help the couple. Instead they quickly went to a nearby resort and alerted Lake Berryessa park rangers. But Hartnell didn't know that was happening. He figured he and Shepard were on their own.

Collecting all the strength he could, Hartnell again tried to crawl toward the road. He'd made it about 300 yards (274 m) to a nearby trail when Park Ranger Dennis Land found him.

"He was lying alongside the dirt road … and I got out and looked at him real quickly," Land said. "He told me his girlfriend was out on the island. As quickly as I could, I got into my car and drove down to where she was."

Ranger Sergeant William White and the owners of Rancho Monticello Resort came to the scene by boat. An ambulance was on its way from the nearest hospital, but that was nearly an hour away. White and Land wrapped the victims in blankets and tried to comfort them. Shepard and Hartnell were scared and in terrible pain, but they tried to tell the rangers all the details they could about the attack.

A little more than an hour after the attack, an officer at the Napa Police Department received a call from a man who wanted to report a double murder at Lake Berryessa.

"I'M THE ONE WHO DID IT."

"I'm the one who did it," the man said, calmly and softly. Again Zodiac had claimed he had killed two people, but he was wrong. Shepard died two days later, but Hartnell survived.

The caller dropped the telephone receiver and walked away without breaking the connection. The officer could hear the sounds of traffic in the background. The call was traced to a car wash pay phone, just a few blocks from the police station. This time Zodiac may have left something behind. Police were able to lift a palm print from the telephone's receiver.

CHAPTER 6

MORE CLUES

apa County Sheriff's Office Detective Sergeant Kenneth Narlow could hardly believe his eyes. The man who had assaulted Cecelia Shepard and Bryan Hartnell had left a message. In black ink on the white door of Hartnell's car, Narlow read:

Vallejo

12-20-68

7-4-69

Sept 27-69-6:30

by knife

Narlow immediately realized what the message meant. The last date and time, and *by knife*, referred to the attack on Shepard and Hartnell. *12-20-68* was the date of the murders of David Faraday and Betty Lou Jensen. *7-4-69* was the night Darlene Ferrin and Mike Mageau were attacked. According to the message, all these crimes were the work of Zodiac. If there was any doubt, the crossed-circle symbol of Zodiac on the door seemed to erase any questions.

The Lake Berryessa assault provided officers with more evidence than the earlier crimes had.

Napa Police Captain Don Townsend covered the message on Hartnell's car door to protect it.

Police had the palm print from the telephone receiver Zodiac used to call the Napa Police Department. They had the writing on the door of Hartnell's car. Officers also found footprints leading to and from the crime scene. They determined that the footprints had been made by size 10½ Wing Walkers, a type of military boot. The depth of the footprints led investigators to believe they were made by a heavy man, perhaps weighing as much as 220 pounds (100 kg).

They also had an eyewitness. Though the killer had been in disguise, Bryan Hartnell had talked to him and could give a general description.

Unfortunately, none of this information would help cabdriver Paul Stine. Just a couple of weeks after the Lake Berryessa attack, Stine picked up Zodiac in San Francisco and drove him to the Presidio Heights neighborhood. As Stine slowed the cab at the address Zodiac had given him, the killer told him to drive another block. It was there that Zodiac shot and killed the cabbie.

After wiping his fingerprints from the cab and taking a piece of the driver's bloody gray and white shirt, Zodiac casually walked away. The teens who had noticed the cab called the police. As Zodiac strolled north on Cherry Street, out of the teens' view, the police hadn't yet arrived.

However, a squad car nearby was headed to the scene. At Jackson and Cherry streets, the officers in the car saw a heavyset white man dressed in dark clothes walking in the direction of the Presidio. They called out to him, asking whether he'd seen

THEY DIDN'T REALIZE THEY PROBABLY HAD JUST TALKED TO ZODIAC.

anything unusual in the last few minutes. The man said he'd seen a man with a gun running east on Washington Street. Thinking that description fit the man they were looking for, the officers rushed toward Washington Street. They didn't realize they probably had just talked to Zodiac.

At first the police dispatcher broadcasting the alert had said the cabbie's killer was a black man. By the time the officers realized the mistake, Zodiac was long gone. He'd probably stashed a getaway car somewhere in the neighborhood near where he had shot Stine.

A new alert went out to police, telling them of the earlier mistake in the suspect's description. K-9 units were brought to the crime scene to hunt for the suspect. A fire department spotlight lit the area.

Homicide Inspector Dave Toschi and his partner, Inspector Bill Armstrong, were roused

Dave Toschi (left) and Bill Armstrong would work on the Zodiac case for years.

from their sleep to help with the investigation. They talked to an officer at the scene. Toschi took out a notebook and jotted down the details of the crime scene. Armstrong walked into the growing crowd and took the names and addresses of witnesses.

THE LAB WORKERS FOUND THE PRINTS OF A RIGHT HAND MADE IN BLOOD.

Soon men from the crime lab joined the inspectors. They dusted the cab for fingerprints. Toschi and Armstrong knew that any prints would have to be checked against Stine's own prints as well as of those of passengers from earlier in the day. Any remaining prints found could very well belong to the killer. Still, they didn't expect to get so lucky. The lab workers found the prints of a right hand made in blood. If they weren't Stine's prints, they almost had to be the prints of the killer.

Cab robberies weren't unusual in San Francisco. Toschi and Armstrong figured this was just one that had gone terribly wrong. However, they soon learned that this was no ordinary robbery and murder. A few days later, Zodiac took credit for the killing in a letter—and unveiled a sinister plan that would spread fear like never before.

THE PRESIDIO

The Presidio was a U.S. Army post just north of Cherry and Washington streets in San Francisco. Unlike many army posts, the Presidio had few areas that were restricted from the public. Police thought Paul Stine's killer could have escaped to the post. They used floodlights and police dogs to thoroughly search the area, but no clues were found. The army closed the Presidio in 1989. It is now a national park.

CHAPTER 7

TAUNTS AND TERROR

It didn't take more than a quick glance at the envelope to see that the letter, which had been marked twice with "Please Rush to Editor," was unusual. A crossed-circle symbol was in the upper left corner of the envelope, where the return address usually goes. The letter was from Zodiac.

It arrived at the *San Francisco Chronicle* October 14, 1969, and included a piece of a bloody shirt. The letter began:

This is the Zodiac speaking. I am the murderer of the taxi driver over by Washington St + Maple St last night, to prove this here is a blood stained piece of his shirt. I am the same man who did the people in the north bay area. The S.F. Police could have caught me last night if they had searched the park properly instead of holding road races with their motorcycles seeing who could make the most noise. The car drivers should have just parked their cars and sat there quietly waiting for me to come out of cover.

This is the Zodiac speaking. I am the murderer of the taxi driver over by Washington St + Maple St last night, to prove this here is a blood stained piece of his shirt. I am the same man who did in the people in the north bay a-ea. The S.F. Police could have caught me last night if they had

A letter from Zodiac arrived at the *Chronicle* October 14, 1969.

Had Zodiac hidden in a nearby park? Witnesses told police they had seen a man matching Zodiac's description running through Julius Kahn Public Playground before disappearing in thick brush in the Presidio. But police and trained dogs had searched the area, checking every tree and shrub. Was Zodiac just taunting them? If he had stashed a car near the Presidio, he could have been gone long before police even began their search.

Zodiac had more in mind than just taunting the police when he sent his letter. He also included a threat:

School children make nice targets, I think I shall wipe out a school bus some morning. Just shoot out the front tire + then pick off the kiddies as they come bouncing out.

After reading the letter, officials at the newspaper immediately called San Francisco police. Toschi recognized the swatch of fabric in the envelope as having come from Stine's shirt.

Toschi realized this crime wasn't an ordinary cab robbery. Zodiac had gone from killing couples in isolated areas to murdering a cabdriver in the heart of the city.

Zodiac seemed to be capable of anything. The threat to kill schoolchildren on a bus could be real. There was no way to know where he would strike. All the killings and assaults so far had been in different areas. There was no pattern.

The *Chronicle* published the first part of Zodiac's letter. Police had asked that the paper not publish the threat against schoolchildren. The *Chronicle* honored the request. Nobody wanted to cause widespread panic, and police needed time to figure out how to handle the situation.

PARENTS WERE TERRIFIED FOR THEIR CHILDREN'S SAFETY.

Soon police decided that people had a right to know about the threat. On October 17 it was made public. Emergency bulletins were sent to schools. Bus drivers were told how to protect themselves and children if they were attacked. In one school district, an extra adult was put on each bus in case Zodiac shot the driver. Police officers, sheriff's deputies, or highway patrol officers also guarded children on buses. Patrol planes flew overhead. Parents were terrified for their children's safety.

DIRTY HARRY

The 1971 Clint Eastwood movie *Dirty Harry* was based on the threat Zodiac made against schoolchildren. In the movie, Eastwood plays Harry Callahan, a San Francisco homicide inspector, who is chasing a crazed sniper called Scorpio. In a letter to San Francisco police, Scorpio threatens to keep killing people until his ransom demands are met. In an effort to secure his ransom, Scorpio kidnaps a school bus full of children. He's no match for Dirty Harry, though, who saves all the students and gets the bad guy.

"THE POLICE SHALL NEVER CATCH ME, BECAUSE I HAVE BEEN TOO CLEVER FOR THEM."

On Monday, November 10, 1969, the *Chronicle* received two more letters from Zodiac. One had been mailed November 8 and the other the next day. The November 8 letter was known as the "Dripping Pen" letter because it was written on a greeting card that showed a dripping pen on the front. Zodiac threatened to kill more people if his messages weren't published. Included with the letter was another cipher, which the newspaper published.

This time, however, no one would be able to break the code.

Perhaps most disturbing was a boast Zodiac made in the letter. He now claimed to have killed seven people—two more than police had connected him to—but he didn't offer any details. Were there really more victims?

Police believed Zodiac was lying. There were no unsolved murders in August 1969, the month Zodiac claimed he'd killed two more victims. In the letter postmarked November 9, he said, "The police shall never catch me, because I have been too clever for them."

Police still followed up any leads they could find that might help them identify Zodiac. They even went to stores that sold greeting cards, hoping to find the place where Zodiac bought the "Dripping Pen" card.

Soon Zodiac would strike again. But this time, luck wouldn't be on his side.

CHAPTER 8

BOTCHED ABDUCTION

Kathy Johns picked up her baby daughter, Jennifer, and put the 10-month-old girl in the station wagon. It was around 7 p.m. on March 22, 1970, and the two were headed for Petaluma, in northern California, about 500 miles (805 km) north of their home in San Bernardino. They were going to visit Johns' sick mother. Johns preferred to make the trip at night. Traveling was easier when the baby slept.

The trip was going fine. Johns was driving along a lonely stretch of Highway 132. In Modesto Johns noticed the headlights of a car following her on the two-lane highway. As she continued past the town, the headlights stayed behind her. Thinking the car's driver wanted to pass, Johns slowed down. But instead of passing her, the car, a light-colored sedan, pulled up alongside hers. Johns saw that the driver was trying to shout something at her through the open passenger-side window. She thought she heard him say that one of her rear wheels was wobbling.

Johns had no intention of stopping on such an isolated stretch of road. The man slowed his car and kept following her until she turned onto Highway 5, a busier road.

Once on Highway 5, Johns pulled to the shoulder of the road. The man who had been following her stopped behind her car. Carrying a lug wrench, he walked to her window. Because the man was dressed well and seemed helpful, Johns accepted his offer to tighten the lug nuts on her wobbly wheel. She was seven months pregnant and didn't relish the thought of having to do it herself. She was grateful for the warning and for the help.

Out of her view, the man worked on the rear wheel, soon returning to tell her the problem was fixed. The man went back to his car and left. Johns drove back onto the highway but soon realized she had a problem. She only traveled a few feet before her right rear wheel came off.

Johns was relieved to see that the man who had helped her had noticed what happened. He came back and looked at the wheel. He offered her a ride to a gas station that could be seen from where they stood. It was near midnight, and the man seemed nice. Johns decided to accept his generosity. She grabbed Jennifer and climbed into the man's car. Suddenly she realized she'd left her key in her car's ignition and the station wagon's lights on. The man went back to her car, shut off the lights, and pocketed her key.

With Johns and her baby in his car, the man drove off, but he didn't stop at the gas station, as he had said he would. At first Johns wasn't alarmed. She thought he had just missed the exit.

"When he missed it, I really didn't think much about it," she said later. "I didn't say anything. When he passed the next exit, it dawned on me something wasn't right. As long as he wasn't talking, neither was I. We went several more exits before he got off, and then I just didn't say anything. He was doing the driving."

When the man turned off the highway and onto a deserted country road, Johns knew she might be in trouble.

"YOU KNOW I'M GOING TO KILL YOU."

"Do you always go around helping people on the road like this?" she asked, obviously upset.

"When I get through with them they don't need any help," he replied. And he kept driving. Johns was sure then that her and her daughter's lives were in danger.

A half hour later, the man spoke again.

"You know you're going to die," he said. "You know I'm going to kill you."

Johns didn't doubt his intentions. She tried to stay calm, looking for a chance to escape. In the meantime, she tried to remember everything about the man that she could. She thought he weighed about 170 pounds (77 kg) and was about 5 feet 9 inches (175 cm) tall. His brown hair was short. He wore a dark blue or black nylon windbreaker and black wool pants. His dark-colored shoes shone. His black glasses were held in place with a band of elastic around the back of his head.

Suddenly Johns saw her chance to escape. The man had accidentally driven up a highway off ramp.

If he continued, he'd be going the wrong way on the highway. He had to stop. When he did, Johns knew she had to make her move.

With Jennifer in her arms, she jumped out of the car, ran across the road, and leaped into an irrigation ditch surrounded by tall grass. She lay as flat as she could, covering Jennifer so the baby wouldn't make a sound and give away their position.

As Johns' heart pounded, a truck driver stopped to see what was going on. The kidnapper raced to his car and left. The trucker came closer to Johns and her daughter. Terribly shaken from her ordeal, she didn't want another strange man coming anywhere near her. He said he understood, and he waited until a female driver came along. The trucker flagged down the car and asked the driver to take Johns and Jennifer to the police station in nearby Patterson.

Safe at the police station, Johns told her terrifying story to an officer. As she spoke, an artist's sketch on the wall caught her eye. It was a sketch of Zodiac drawn after Paul Stine's murder. It looked like the man who had just abducted her.

If anyone doubted Johns' story, they'd soon have proof. Zodiac took credit for the abduction in a July 1970 letter to the *Chronicle*.

WANTED

SAN FRANCISCO POLICE DEPARTMENT

NO. 90-69   WANTED FOR MURDER   OCTOBER 18, 1969

ORIGINAL DRAWING   AMENDED DRAWING

Supplementing our Bulletin 87-69 of October 13, 1969. Additional information has developed the above amended drawing of murder suspect known as "ZODIAC".

WMA, 35-45 Years, approximately 5'8", Heavy Build, Short Brown Hair, possibly with Red Tint, Wears Glasses. Armed with 9 mm Automatic.

Available for comparison: Slugs, Casings, Latents, Handwriting.

ANY INFORMATION:
Inspectors Armstrong & Toschi
Homicide Detail   THOMAS J. CAHILL
CASE NO. 696314   CHIEF OF POLICE

Kathy Johns spotted a similar poster in the Patterson police station.

CHAPTER 9

DISAPPEARING ACT

For years after the abduction of Johns and her daughter, Zodiac occasionally sent letters to the *Chronicle* claiming more victims. Police thought he might be taking credit for murders committed by others. Zodiac didn't give specific information about the crimes, as he had done in the past. He may have stopped killing, but he still seemed to enjoy taunting the police.

Between March 1971 and January 1974, Zodiac was silent. Police didn't know whether he was dead, in jail, or in a mental institution. Perhaps he'd moved away. But a new letter in 1974 mentioning the horror movie *The Exorcist* made authorities believe Zodiac was still around. And the public wanted to help catch him.

"Since the latest Zodiac letter was published, I've had 50 people in my office," inspector Dave Toschi said in 1974. "Each claims he knows Zodiac personally. Bill [Armstrong] and I have probably followed up 1,000 leads in this case and heard a lot

This is the Zodiac speaking

I have become very upset with the people of San Fran Bay Area. They have <u>not</u> complied with my wishes for them to wear some nice ⊕ buttons. I promiced to punish them if they did not comply, by anilating a full School Bass. But now schod is out for the sammer, so I punished them in an another way. I shot a man sitting in a parked car with a .38.

⊕-12   SFPD-0

The Map coupled with this code will tell you where the bomb is set. You have antill next Fall to dig it up. ⊕

C △ J I ■ O K ⅃ A M ⅂ ▲ Ω O R T ⌀
X ⊙ F D V ⸂ ▣ H C E L ⊕ P W △

A June 1970 letter was one of many sent by Zodiac.

of weird stories. People tell us they're sure it's their neighbor because he looks like the drawing and walks around with a knife in a scabbard. ... There are times when you're listening to this and it's hard to keep a straight face. But I feel I've got to listen to everyone, no matter how outlandish their story is."

Zodiac mailed four letters to the *San Francisco Chronicle* in 1974. After that, nothing was heard from him for four years. As leads dried up, fewer police were assigned to the case. By the mid-1970s, Toschi was the only investigator still assigned to it.

In April 1978 Zodiac sent what turned out to be his final letter to the *Chronicle.* It was a threatening, bragging letter, like those that had come before it. But the writer seemed more deeply disturbed than before.

By 1981 the case was considered all but closed. It was turned over to the California State Department of Justice, in Sacramento. Toschi, who had been involved in the case since Paul Stine's murder, wasn't happy with this decision. Even though he'd been

"SO, I CAN NEVER GET AWAY FROM THE ZODIAC CASE, AND I DO NOT THINK I EVER WILL."

moved to the Robbery Division in July 1978, people still associated Toschi with Zodiac and contacted him with tips on the case.

"So, I can never get away from the Zodiac case, and I do not think I ever will," he said. "It's become part of my life—on and off duty."

Toschi retired in 1985 after 32 years on the force, but he never got over Zodiac.

"I still consider the Zodiac case the most frustrating of all my cases," he said when he retired. "I really believe it gave me bleeding ulcers."

Despite all the evidence they collected, police were never able to use it to connect anyone to the crimes. For instance, they could not find a match to the bloody print found in Paul Stine's cab, the palm print in the phone booth, or the fingerprints on a letter sent by Zodiac. Though Zodiac enclosed three pieces of Stine's bloody shirt in letters, the rest of the shirt remains missing.

There have been many theories. One was that Zodiac or one of his parents was from the United Kingdom, Australia, or South Africa. In some letters he used terms more common in those countries, such as "blue meanies," referring to police.

More than 2,500 people were considered potential suspects at one time or another, but all were cleared. Among the most likely was a man named Arthur Leigh Allen. A resident of Vallejo and a convicted child molester, Allen is said to have claimed he was Zodiac. But when police compared his fingerprints with those found on Paul Stine's cab, they discovered there was no match.

AN EARLIER VICTIM?

Zodiac was a suspect in several other murders. One was that of Cheri Jo Bates.

Bates was an 18-year-old student at Riverside City College in Riverside, California, when she was stabbed to death October 30, 1966. Bates was walking to her car from the college library about 9:30 that evening when someone stabbed her in an alley. Her body was found the next morning.

Bates' murder was similar to the Zodiac killings in several ways. The weapon was a knife, and footprints of a man's size 8 to 10 shoe were found at the scene. Most tellingly, the Riverside police and the local newspaper both received letters from a person confessing to the crime in November 1966. Other letters were mailed in April 1967 to the police, the newspaper, and Bates' father. Also, a poem about stabbing was carved into a desk at the college library sometime in December 1966.

In March 1971 Zodiac sent a letter to the *Los Angeles Times* taking credit for Bates' murder. Police believe he wrote that letter, the 1967 letters, and the poem on the desk. However, they don't think he was the killer. They believe a former boyfriend of Bates killed her, but they don't have enough evidence to charge him.

When Allen died in 1992, some people close to the Zodiac investigation still thought he might have been the killer. But an analysis of DNA evidence in 2002 seemed to clear him. The DNA in saliva on an envelope sent by Zodiac didn't match Allen's DNA. Still, some people remain convinced that he was guilty.

It's possible that Zodiac remains at large today. "I still think Zodiac is out there someplace," Captain Ken Narlow of the Napa County Sheriff's Office said in late 1978. "I sometimes look out the window and wonder how close we've come to him at times. We rattled so many cages and kicked so many bushes along the way, we must have been near him at least once."

Some police believe that if Zodiac had died, relatives going through his belongings would have found evidence of his identity. Perhaps they'd have found the hood he wore at Lake Berryessa or copies of letters and ciphers similar to those written by Zodiac. But even if that had happened, the family may not have wanted to bring the evidence to anyone's attention.

Some people have said a family member was the Zodiac killer. In April 2009 Deborah Perez told reporters that her dead father, Guy Ward Hendrickson, had been Zodiac. She gave police what she believed were Paul Stine's glasses and letters she said her father had made her write to newspapers for him. The police examined her evidence but didn't find it credible.

While most people don't believe such stories, there are other theories. One is that Zodiac was mentally ill. When he reached his mid-30s, his rage may have burned out. He could have lived the rest of his life without killing. He might not even have remembered being Zodiac. But this is just a theory.

No matter what happened to Zodiac, the fascination with him continues. Books and Internet sites detail his crimes and the investigation. In 2007 the movie *Zodiac* was released and did well at the box office.

Deborah Perez (center) claimed her dead father had been the Zodiac Killer.

Eddie Seda copied the Zodiac's crimes during a killing spree in the 1990s.

Unfortunately, the fascination with Zodiac isn't always healthful. A copycat killer struck in New York City in the 1990s, killing three people and injuring five more. During his killing spree, the killer sent letters to the police written in a manner similar to Zodiac's and signed with the Zodiac symbol. Police arrested the copycat, Heriberto "Eddie" Seda, in 1996. In 1998 he was convicted and sentenced to 232 years in prison.

Victims who survived attacks by the Zodiac copycat in New York, as well as the victims' families, carry physical and emotional scars. But Seda's capture and eventual conviction at least gave them some closure. Those involved in the Zodiac case in California don't even have that—and they probably never will.

THE UNABOMBER—AND ZODIAC?

A former professor and convicted terrorist, Theodore Kaczynski, was once thought to be the Zodiac killer. Nicknamed the Unabomber, Kaczynski was arrested in 1996 in Montana after a series of mail bombings that killed three people and injured 23. He was sentenced to life in prison without the possibility of parole. Kaczynski was cleared in the Zodiac killings when police discovered his fingerprints did not match those in the Zodiac case file.

TIMELINE

October 30
1966
Cheri Jo Bates is murdered in Riverside, California. The crime is similar to those of Zodiac's, but the police eventually decided that he was not her killer.

December 20
1968
Zodiac murders Betty Lou Jensen and David Faraday in Vallejo, California.

July 4
1969
Zodiac kills Darlene Ferrin and injures Michael Mageau in Vallejo.

July 31
1969
Zodiac sends letters and parts of a cipher to three California newspapers.

August 4

1969 Donald and Bettye Harden solve Zodiac's first cipher.

September 27

1969 Zodiac attacks Cecelia Shepard and Bryan Hartnell at Lake Berryessa; Hartnell survives, but Shepard dies two days later.

October 11

1969 Zodiac murders Paul Stine in San Francisco, California.

October 14

1969 The *San Francisco Chronicle* receives the first of several letters Zodiac sends late in 1969 and into the 1970s.

TIMELINE

March 22

1970
Zodiac abducts Kathy Johns and her baby daughter, Jennifer, near Modesto, California. They are able to escape.

April 24

1978
Zodiac sends his final letter to the *San Francisco Chronicle*.

March 8 **October 2**

1990-1993
Copycat killer Heriberto "Eddie" Seda kills three people and wounds five in separate attacks in New York City. He is captured in 1996 and convicted and sentenced to 232 years in prison in 1998.

August 26

1992 Arthur Leigh Allen, considered by many to be the prime suspect in the Zodiac killings, dies in Vallejo, California.

October

2002 DNA evidence clears Arthur Leigh Allen.

2007 The movie *Zodiac*, starring Mark Ruffalo, Robert Downey Jr., and Jake Gyllenhaal, is released.

April 29

2009 At a news conference, California real estate agent Deborah Perez claims that her dead father, Guy Ward Hendrickson, had been Zodiac. Few people believe her.

GLOSSARY

afterlife—existence after death

cipher—a coded message

dispatcher—a person who sends messages to police officers on a police radio

DNA—the molecule that carries the genetic code that gives living things their individual characteristics; DNA stands for deoxyribonucleic acid

illuminate—to light

peninsula—a piece of land jutting into a body of water

scabbard—a sheath for a knife

signature—a handwritten name; also a logo or mark used to set apart or identify

skeptical—doubtful

ADDITIONAL RESOURCES

READ MORE

Editors of *Life* magazine. *Life: Greatest Unsolved Mysteries of All Time*. New York: Life Books, 2009.

Newton, Michael. *The Encyclopedia of Serial Killers*. New York: Facts on File, 2006.

Newton, Michael. *Serial Killers*. New York: Chelsea House Publishers, 2008.

Yancey, Diane. *The Case of the Zodiac Killer*. Detroit: Lucent Books, 2008.

Yancey, Diane. *Tracking Serial Killers*. Farmington Hills, Mich.: Lucent Books: Thomson/Gale, 2007.

INTERNET SITES

Use FactHound to find Internet sites related to this book. All of the sites on FactHound have been researched by our staff.

Here's all you do:
Visit *www.facthound.com*
Type in this code: 9780756543570

SELECT BIBLIOGRAPHY

About Zodiac Killer. 15 March 2010. www.zodiackiller.com/About.html

Chronicle and SFGate staff. The Zodiac Killer in Print. *San Francisco Chronicle*. 25 Feb. 2007. 15 March 2010. www.sfgate.com/cgi-bin/article.cgi?f=/c/a/2007/02/25/PKzodiacpages25.DTL

Crowley, Kieran. *Sleep My Little Dead: The True Story of the Zodiac Killer*. New York: St. Martin's Paperbacks, 1997.

Graysmith, Robert. *Zodiac*. New York: St. Martin's/Marek, 1986.

Graysmith, Robert. *Zodiac Unmasked: The Identity of America's Most Elusive Serial Killer Revealed*. New York: Berkley Books, 2002.

Kelleher, Michael D., and David Van Nuys. *"This Is the Zodiac Speaking": Into the Mind of a Serial Killer*. Westport, Conn.: Praeger, 2002.

McKinley, Jesse. "Californian Says Father Was Zodiac Killer." *The New York Times*. 29 April 2009. 15 March 2010. www.nytimes.com/2009/04/30/us/30zodiac.htm

Secrets of the Dead. 15 March 2010. www.pbs.org/wnet/secrets/executed-in-error/perennial-thrillers-murder-mystery-obsession

Still Searching for the Zodiac Killer. ABC News. 20 Feb. 2007. 15 March 2010. http://abcnews.go.com/Primetime/Story?id=2889679&page=1

The Zodiac Killer. 15 March 2010. www.trutv.com/library/crime/serial_killers/notorious/zodiac/river_1.html

Zodiac Killer Biography. 15 March 2010. www.biography.com/articles/Zodiac-Killer-236027

INDEX

ABOUT THE AUTHOR

Brenda Haugen started in the newspaper business and had a career as an award-winning journalist before finding her niche as an author. Since then, she has written and edited many books, most of them for children. A graduate of the University of North Dakota in Grand Forks, Brenda lives in North Dakota with her family.